Danmar Chuan Dao: Complete P. ... .
By Dan Marson

Acknowledgements

A special thanks to Aurelio Lopez, a dear friend and author of the photos that made this book possible. And to all my students from around the world, including China, that saw my value, respected me and shown curiosity for my knowledge, while allowing me to improve with their questions, interests and motivation. This book is a result of such entire dynamic and their aspirations for more and better in the field of martial arts.

Also, a special thank you to all the Martial Artists and friends that have helped me see beyond the techniques of any style, and understand the true meaning of kung fu, while showing me the roots of Chinese martial arts and philosophy. They have supported me in this quest and have gladly and kindly insisted in the conception of this book with pride for my representation of a new and modern kung fu style.

It is my great honor to have known all those amazing people and to receive the approval of all the Chinese nationals that I've met in the promotion of my system of combat and training as a new branch of kung fu.

Table of Contents

Introduction

Dan Mar Chuan Dao Kung Fu, or in Chinese language Dān Mǎ Quán Dào Gōng Fu, is a modern style of kung fu, developed throughout several years of interaction with different kung fu Sifus in China, from north to south, in which there were new learnings and teachings from both sides, not only in the technical field but also, and foremost, philosophical.

The Chinese characters for this martial art are represented as 丹马拳道功夫, accurately meaning the Boxing Way of Dan in Kung Fu.The word kung fu is Cantonese, meaning good technique or good performance, and it was because Danmar ChuanDao was popularized and widely taught in this province to a large amount of students that this definition was chosen.

In this book, you have the complete training program with charts and images to practice on your own, and also create a group of followers. It includes pictures and descriptions for stances, movements, forms, attacks, defenses and grapples. but also for warm-up exercises and energy healing practices based on Chi Gong principles.

This is a modern martial art created for the modern world, but based in ancient Chinese philosophies and culture, and can be practiced by anyone, with or without any background in the martial arts, as a way to improve health, discipline, coordination, focus and good self-defense habits.

Learning and Teaching TaiChi

My experience with Tai Chi taught me about the importance of having a strong body, but the greatest lesson came, not when I started practicing, but years later, when my Chinese doctor, also a Tai Chi Master, performed a healing on me by applying his ability to control chi in my body. It was a moment in which I deeply felt the importance of martial arts, far beyond what anyone can see or understand within his own mind.

Later I had a chance to apply these principles by myself, when an accident in the south of China made me dislocate my shoulder. The doctor used acupuncture in the first day and said I would need several months to recover, and might not even fully recover. But the previous experience with chi taught me otherwise and, by using my own exercises, I was fully recovered, to his amazement, after only two days.

Indeed doctors can teach and learn, and in-between I gained something very valuable about the mechanics of the body.

This knowledge, along with all these experiences, was incorporated in my martial art, in exercises and techniques that promote inner strength, more than outer strength. I have specifically organized them as routines that can easily be followed, just as kung fu masters did in the past with their styles.

Learning and Teaching Wushu

Wushu, the fighting style of the north of China, shown me a mixture of beauty and power. But, more importantly, how to coordinate them effectively.

Until then, despite having already two decades of my life dedicated to martial arts, I thought that you can either practice a soft or a hard style in martial arts but not both. Today, even though I can't explain it to anyone that hasn't experienced the same as me, I know that there's no such thing as one type of martial art or another. This illusion disguises the true meaning of practicing kung fu, which is to understand the flow from strength and domain to weakness and vulnerability, without choosing one or the other. It is the path of tao, by knowing yin and yang, and then find zen, a state in which there's no ego, but only being.

I ended up incorporating this lesson in my training strategies, which then became part of the application and flow of techniques in Danmar Kung Fu. But I also understood this lesson well enough to be invited for a regional performance of martial arts in the north of China. A sign of appreciation for my efforts in bridging east and west, a sign of respect for my fast improvements in applying this philosophy to martial arts and life, to all those around me, and, above anything else, a chance to show to everyone that, despite their background or appearance, there's much to learn in what makes us similar. Truly, a lesson to everyone that knew me for an entire year, and couldn't even imagine that me, a peaceful, quiet and friendly individual, would do the demonstration that I did in front of a vast audience of hundreds of Chinese and foreigners from different nationalities. In that day, I didn't wear any uniform, because that's what made this experience far more special for everyone, specially when I grabbed and used the weapons.

Learning and Teaching Sanda

The final stage of my journey, before the final compilation of knowledge was presented in the form of a complete martial art, happened in Guangzhou, the Cantonese capital of China. I was practicing and learning different styles of kung fu at the same time, until one day I noticed in the surrounding area a tree shaking with the punches and kicks of a young boy. Curious about it, I approached him to know what he was really doing. Then, one thing led to another, and after that day we were practicing together his own interpretation of kung fu. He also explained to me the difference between traditional and modern interpretations of kung fu. It was him that shown me that you don't need a fancy gym and a punching bag to practice martial arts regularly and become good at it.

This boy, named Jifasu, aka. The Rock, reminded me a lot of Bruce Lee. He talked like him, thought like him and was just as much addicted to training as Bruce Lee was. In fact, it was thanks to him that I started understanding the principles that Bruce Lee was trying to show in his Jeet Kune Do. He had a part-time job as a security guard, so I believe he knew what he was trying to achieve with his training.

Nevertheless, I did found a way to enrich his practice, with techniques I had learned in other countries, namely, with Masters in the Philippines. So, a few months after we started practicing together, there were dozens of people wanting to practice with us as well. Naturally, due to the huge amount of techniques I was putting into the training and my experience as an instructor, it became normal to start teaching everyone on my own, that boy included. But I didn't know what to call that unique kung fu style every time someone asked me about it. I also couldn't explain precisely this entire story in a way that could easily be understood. Therefore, I decided to call it Daniel Kung Fu, which was a name practitioners could recognize well. That's how Danmar Kung Fu was born.

It is amazing how everything evolved and how I became a kung fu instructor in China and with Chinese students. But, probably more surprised than me was a shaolin monk that visited us once to train with everyone and said that, among all the foreigners and Chinese he had trained with, I was the first he had met that truly understands the meaning of kung fu.

My journey in China and with kung fu continued then in Shanghai, with other Sifus, but at that point I felt that I already had enough experience to guarantee Danmar Kung Fu as a solid and effective martial art, so not much was changed. This manual resumes a path that has no limits, but must be found by each one that chooses to pursue it.

I have given several guidelines along the book to help the reader practice on his own, and without the need for an instructor guiding him. It's a simple martial art based on very ancient principles, but also easy to learn.

The Roots of DK

During my entire life, I've tried to find a martial art that could be efficient and at the same time fun to practice, but I've never found it.

I've been an instructor of Kickboxing, MuayThai, Filipino Martial Arts, Medieval Fighting, Kempo, Capoeira, Jeet Kune Do and Self-defense. And, apart from these martial arts, I also had several Instructors from others, such as Krav Maga, wanting to improve their knowledge with me.

Within my background, can be found as well the training of police officers and security guards, public demonstrations in different countries, and talk-shows in famous radios.

As I progressed in the field of martial arts, I felt trapped in dogmas and misunderstandings, which, despite my recognition and popularity among martial artists, I couldn't deal with easily. So, most of my training started progressing independently and with the use of weapons. At that time, I was practicing every night, and with any weapon I could find, although my favorite were the most difficult to use, namely, the rope-dart and the balisong. Finally, however, I decided to focus on the katana, because it helped me explore a new form of harmony in the practice of combat.

From this daily experience in the use of weapons, I started creating a model of empty-hand training that would later become the basis of all the knowledge incorporated from my experience in China.

The Goals of DK

There's no such thing as a perfect martial art. It's, basically, impossible to train for every situation possible and while maintaining different philosophical goals. Within these limitations, we may extend our practice, but we either train to defend or to attack, otherwise we are training to think, which doesn't quite work when you're nervous.

Time is also limited, so we either spend it practicing with weapons, or without them but, even among the techniques chosen, our improvements can be measured by our dedication to each. In today's world, people lack time and patience, and most of the times they don't have enough motivation to dedicate themselves to a discipline that will only bring them fruits many years later.

In conclusion, Danmar Kung Fu isn't a perfect martial art and doesn't intend to be. It merely simplifies a personal experience, insights and beliefs, that were compiled in a simple to follow program, that enhances focus, health, effective techniques and a good fighting strategy. Besides, contrary to many modern martial arts, intends to be intuitive, natural for the body and mind, and logic as well. The pattern of training presented here was built in a way that can easily be adopted by anyone, from any age range, and in any environment. It can be practiced outdoors or at home, by a young person or an older individual.

Why DK is a Futuristic Martial Art

Danmar Kung Fu was created for an individual to be able to practice alone, but it's not limited to such training method. In fact, as a person expands in his personal experience with this martial art, will eventually perceive new ways of applying it. Those new ways can be found in other methods of training.

When DK (Danmar Kung Fu) was planned, it was thought within the following possible applications, which, unfortunately, I have personally faced in real life situations, and from which I escaped alive, without any injury or even a scratch, thanks to this martial art that has saved my life many times.

- Fighting against multiple opponents;

- Defending without fighting back;

- Fighting against stronger and taller opponents;

- Controlling an attacker without using violence;

- Facing knifes;

- Avoiding an imminent fight, simply by using the right body position.

- Training the previous situations alone.

DK also takes into account personal perspectives about self-defense in the modern world, such as:

- The fact that violence is always present in unpredictable forms, even for the most experienced self-defense instructors;

- Statistics show that usually you're attacked in the most vulnerable situation;

- Disadvantage in a street fighting is very common;

- Self-protection is limited by law, and often the criminal can be confused with the victim;

- Learning in a class takes too much time before you feel able to protect yourself;

- Most people can't afford to pay for self-defense classes;

• Most people are attacked indoors and not outdoors;

• Many people are attacked by someone they know;

• Most people are attacked because they don't want to fightback;

• Many people would prefer to practice self-defense privately.

Above all these needs, in today's world, you need to be a master of yourself, as development in a class takes too much time until you can feel that you can defend yourself and your loved ones. Besides, you have to find your own way, not only in fighting but in all aspect of life. Walking a path of self-knowledge and self-conscience is an important ability to acquire.

Apart from this, during moments of war and revolutions, only martial arts that can be practiced alone can survive and become popular, as it's unlikely that anyone will be available to teach others.

The experience of teaching DK to people from different nationalities, on the other hand, led to

the need for the conception of a specific language and codification that can be learned by anyone. And this specificity greatly helps in transforming DK into a technology that permits the reader to learn to master himself and even share his
experience with others. In fact, it could also help
an engineer create a robot for war if needed, because it's based on the same principles of bio-
mechanics.

Why You Can Practice Alone

Years ago, before DK was created, I was told by a famous North American Instructor that teaches martial arts for more than forty years, including the army and MMA fighters, the following: "Nobody can seriously learn a martial art on his own and specially if the founder is only 31 years old and doesn't have as much experience as me". In the end, he suggested to be part of his long-distance training instructors.

My answer to him was the following: "Thank you for answering my email, as I'm nobody in the martial arts world compared to you and cannot even try to compare my own path in martial arts with yours, whose achievements are indeed impressive. Nonetheless, I would like to remember you that you teach a martial art created by a person with the same age as me – Bruce Lee Jeet Kune Do. Besides, it's interesting to notice that you don't believe in me creating a martial art for individual practice but you believe in a long-distance program for solo training created by you. Please think about what I just said".

We can consider this dialogue to make our own conclusions, but what better way there is to understand a culture than living it from inside? In

China, I made many Chinese friends that practice kung fu on their own, firmly believe in their methods and won't consider other forms of practicing it. And I also studied extensively the cultural background and fighting styles of the Chinese, apart from challenging many of them to fight me and test my martial art. I can't say that I won, as that wouldn't be sufficient for me, but I can say that they all quit before I could be defeated, which in China is basically the same as winning. These challenges brought me a profound insight about how Chinese people fight and the application of kung fu in practical ways.

In order to help the student of DK self-correct himself, the practice includes the use of ropes and trees as a support to his awareness regarding how to apply every single defense or attack, but also when learning how to move his body during a fight.

Moral Code

The following list incorporates the philosophy behind DK. One thing cannot be left without the other. Without its philosophy, DK has no meaning and may not serve its purposes. If somebody is teaching this martial art, he must make sure his students know and repeat this list in their classes.

- I won't fight unless I have no other choice;

- I will never submit to fear. I will train hard in order to overcome it;

- When without a choice, I will attack, verbally or physically;

- There's no limit to my training, body and mind, apart from what I decide;

- I am who I choose to be and I can do what I choose to do;

- In a fight, I'll try to finish it quickly without hurting the other person;

- A real champion wins without fists or violence;

- If I have to use my fists to win, I will be fast and hit severely;

- I won't give my opponent any chance to fightback or even think about it;

- If I'm hit and hurt, pain won't stop me from winning or protecting myself;

- If I lose a fight, I win time and experience to prepare for the next;

- A fighter that survives lives to fight another day;

- A fighter that wins a fight is prepared for bigger challenges;

- Courage and integrity are my highest goals;

- I will face the consequences of my actions with integrity;

- Once a decision is made, in any moment, there's no more regret or guilt;

- For the protection of oneself and others, no technique is less suitable;

- I won't judge others but I won't submit to the judgment of others as well;

- I will follow my heart to achieve the ultimate peace within, not pride;

- My worse enemy is my mind, which can lead to fear and confusion;

- My worse mistake as a martial artist is to become arrogant;

- The purpose of my training is the development of my mind;

- I will train to obtain peace in my heart, a healthy body, a strong spirit, a strong will and become a prominent warrior in all aspects of life;

- I will always respect the founder and all my superiors in this martial art;

- I will treat the ones with less knowledge than me with kindness;

- I will help those in need and promote the highest values in society;

- Whenever in doubt, I will follow my instincts and heart;

- I will always look at my present in order to face responsibilities regarding my future;

- I will always choose fast and quickly and face responsibilities for my decisions;

- I practice to become more human, kind, valuable and trustworthy;

- I will always respect all manifestations of life in nature and will refrain from killing, unless I have no other choice possible;

- I will honor my Masters, these values and Danmar Kung Fu.

Training Strategies

As DK is a martial programmed for individual training, the program can be entirely applied in the following ways:

1. Training with a rope;

2. Training with a door entrance;

3. Training with a wall;

4. Training with a tree;

5. Training blindfolded.

The applications used in this book, although using the tree as a reference, can be trained in many different ways, according to the methods described.

Codes for Techniques and Movements

The following list displays the total amount of techniques and movements in DK, as well as the codes attributed to each. These codes will later help in studying the vast array of possible applications.

Action: An action can be an attack, defense, evasive or grappling.

A – Attack (Jing Gong)

D – Defense (Fang Shou)

E – Evasive (Duo Bi)

G - Grappling (Qin Na)

Level: There are 3 levels in the body for either attacking or defending:

1. The head, including the neck (Tou)

2. The body, including the genitals (Shen)

3. The legs, including the knees and feet (Tui)

Side: Side refers to where the action of the fighter is coming from, being it either left, right or both.

    1. Right (Yòu Biān)

    2. Left (Zuǒ Biān)

    3. Both (Shuāng Fāng)

Body: The body code is related to which part of the body will be used for the attack or defense, but it can also include a weapon.

P. Punching hand (Shǒu) or open hand (Dǎkāi Shǒu) for defenses

F. Foot (Jiǎo)

E. Elbow (Zhou)

K. Knee (Xīgài)

H. Head (Tóu)

W. Weapon (Wǔqì)

Angle: An angle refers to one of the 5 lines of movement that can be described with a + or an x.

1. Descending in a straight line (+) - Zhi-Xian XiangXia

2. Descending in diagonal (X) - DuiJiao-Xian XiangXia

3. Horizontal to the floor (+) - Shui Ping

4. Ascending in diagonal(X) - DuiJiaoXian XiangShang

5. Ascending in a straight line (+) - ZhiXi-an XiangShang

Movement: There are 3 directions in which to move for an attack, defense or evasive, and they are based on triangular movements.

1. Triangular movement to the right side (SanJiaoXing XiangYou)

2. Triangular movement to the left side (SanJiaoXing XiangZuo)

3. Moving forward (Xiang Qian)

You should move constantly to the right and left every time you throw a sequence of moves, special when practicing alone.

Stances and Movements

Zi Shi (The Archer): is the primordial stance from which you start your training and execute any technique, when when attacking, defending and evading. It helps you measure distances and position your body according to the following movements that you intend to do. The rope is maintained in the exact length of the stretched arm, starting in the front hand and finishing in the hand protecting the chin. Although this is the basic stance from which all movements are executed and practiced using a rope, without it, and specially during free sparring, the fighter should be flexible enough with his arms and maintain the front arm (either left of right) in a position that easily allows him to control his opponent, keep distance, attack and defend.

Shou Shi (Farming the Land): is the movement your perform with your arm when executing a technique. During this movement, make sure to start and end with one of the hands protecting your chin, and keep the rope stretched. When doing the clockwork movement with your arms, remember to rotate them close to your head. In the middle of this rotation you have one of the defensive techniques, namely, the elbow evasive and the elbow defense, allowing you to almost simultaneously attack and defend. This is a basic movement used for punching, defending and elbowing.

Bō (The Wave): This is an evasive applied by moving the head down in a circular movement with the purpose of avoiding side attacks to the head. It's also used to move safely into the safe area of an opponent to attack him.

Duo Bi (Dodging): is a defensive reaction in which you move your torso either to the right (Duǒbiyou) or the left (Duǒbizuǒ). This is a defensive reaction against punches and firearms in which you move away from the line of attack.

HouTui (Avoiding): is a backward movement of the torso. It consists in moving backwards to avoid straight attacks. You must practice it in a way in which you don't lose balance and can reposition quickly.

Tuī (Pushing): This reaction forces the opponent to create distance, allowing us to strategically put him in the line of a premeditated technique. It can also be used in the opposite manner, such as by pulling (Lā), in which we reposition the opponent and us at the same time within a more convenient line of attack. This technique can also be used to control an attacker, as once in a safe distance we can keep him there with our feet, without the need to start a fight.

Wài BaoZhou DuoBi (Outside)

Nei BaoZhou DuoBi (Inside)

BaoZhou DuoBi (Evasive with elbow): is an evasive movement of the torso in which you simultaneously raise the elbow to protect yourself in a situation of close quarter combat. The elbow evasive is a quick body reaction applied by raising the elbow for close quarter combat, especially when in situations of multiple-attackers. It may be applied to go outside of the opponent angle of attack or to go inside it, depending on the situation.

Attacks

Attacks with the hand are applied by using it like a hammer (chuí), except when the hand is open like a knife (dāo), in which the fingers are used for the attack. In both situations, the hand can be used with either the palm upward or downward and in all previously described angles. This movement can be used and practiced with im-provised weapons as well, such as the coin or a pen. It applies in the angles of action 2 and 3 for levels 1 and 2, as exemplified in the pictures.

Xiàngshàng Chuí (Palm Up) - Level 1 & 2

Xiàngshàng Chuí - Angle 2

Xiàngxià Chuí (Palm Down) - Level 1 & 2

Xiàngxià Chuí - Angle 2

Wài Chuí (hitting like a hammer with the outside of the hand) and **Zhang Chuí** (hitting like a hammer with the inside of the hand) are the most important punches and are applied for level 1 and 2.

Xiàngshàng Dāo (hand like knife with palm upward) or **Xiàngxià Dāo** (hand like knife with palm downward) is applied with the hand open to hit with the fingers at the throat or eyes of the opponent.

Attacks with the foot (jiǎo) can be applied using the outside (Wai Jiǎo), inside (Nei Jiǎo), chest (Xiōngbù Jiǎo) or heel (Jiǎogēn Jiǎo). They're applied as demonstrated in the pictures, mostly for levels 1 and 2. This attack intends to hit the knee of the opponent to stop him or incapacitate him.

Other forms of attacking include the elbow (Zhou), the knee (Xīgài) and the head (Tóu).

If you don't feel comfortable in using these techniques in a tree at the beginning, you can use protections to avoid getting hurt. The most suitable angle of attack for elbow is 2 and for knee is 4, specially if practicing against a wall, because certain angles may cause injury during practice, unless used in a punching bag or with a training partner.

Zhou techniques can be trained with a rope as shown in the picture. Move one of the arms up to protect your head while attacking with the elbow and then alternate between arms while keeping the rope stretched.

Tóu attacks intend to hit the head, nose or chin of the opponent when in close range. It's more suitable for angles 1, 2 and 3 and for levels 1 and 2. The pictures describe attacks using angles 3 and 1.

Other attacks that can be applied are the Hòu,or attacks to your back. The pictures describe some examples.

Defenses

Defenses: Defenses are usually done with the hand open (shǒukāi), although closed hand defenses can be applied as well. You can defend both with the outside (Wai Shou) and inside (Zhang Shou) of the hand.

You can also defend using the inside of your feet (**Nei Jiao**) or the outside (**Wai Jiao**), as well as the elbow (**Wai Jiao**) and the knee (**xīgài**).

Zhou Fángyù Is a defense applied with the elbow, either inside or outside of the angle of attack. The purpose is to counterattack the hands and arms of our attacker, although it can also be used as an attack to the chest and head.

Nei Xīgài Fángyù (defending inside with knee) and **Wai Xīgài Fángyù**(defending outside with knee) are applied to defend the legs, although shouldn't be a prioritized technique. Instead, students of DK should focus on movements and sequences more than defenses.

Wài Jiǎo Fángyù (defending outside with foot) and **Nei Jiǎo Fángyù** (defending inside with foot) are techniques to stop the opponent or his lower attacks.

Grapples and Locks

Qínná (Grappling) is applied not only to hold your opponent with locks but also to escape when grabbed. They are applied to wrists (Wàn), arms (Gēbó), neck (Bózi) and even shirt (Chènshān), and the correct form of how to do it can be trained alone as well. To train these moves, grab your wrist, arm, neck or shirt strongly with the opposite hand.

65

Wan Quinna: The technique in these pictures is used for situations in which the wrist is grabbed. The movement for escaping must be applied for the opposite side as shown in the picture, followed by a counter-attack applied as a punch, fingers to the eyes or pushing away the opponent. However, if you choose to keep the lock on, then you have here one of the most simple and effective arm locks. You may ask somebody else to grab you in order to test the efficiency of your training.

Gebo Quinna: To escape in this situation, you must move your body to the opposite side as shown in the picture, following with a counter-attack.

Bozl Qulnna: This technique is used for situations in which the neck is grabbed. To escape, you must turn to the same side as the hand grabbing you, finishing with a counter-attack.

Chenshan Quinna: This technique is used for situations in which a shirt or jacket is grabbed. To escape, you must control the arm of the opponent and then move it backwards, while pulling it in the same direction of our body. This technique can be applied quickly, if we twist our body in the same direction of the hand of our opponent, as shown in the picture for Bozi Quinna. However, if we don't let the opponent go, it can finish as an arm lock that can make him submisse, and even go to the floor.

Furthermore, despite what anyone might think about these techniques, I must say that they are crucial in DK, simply because they have saved my life many times, and in many countries, often against multiple and stronger attackers. They allow you to stop opponents without giving them a chance of fighting back. If you can dominate well the Quinna techniques, which can also be used to attack and not only defend, you may never need to really fight anyone, as there will not be time or opportunity for any punch or kick to occur. What you train alone are the correct reactions, so that you may respond quickly and effectively in a crucial situation without even thinking about it. You must see it as a mental programming.

Applications

The following list covers the applications to be trained.

Attacks (Jìng Gōng): Attacks can be applied in 3 levels and within 3 angles.

- Xiàngshàng Chuí: Level 1, 2 / Angle 2, 3
- Xiàngxià Chuí: Level 1, 2 / Angle 2, 3,4
- Wài Chuí: Level 1, 2 / Angle 1, 2, 3
- Zhang Chuí: Level 1, 2 / Angle 2, 3, 4, 5
- Xiàngshàng Dāo: Level 1/ Angle 1,5
- Xiàngxià Dāo: Level 1/ Angle 1,5
- Wài Jiǎo: Level 1,2,3/ Angle 2,3,4
- Zhang Jiǎo: Level 2,3/ Angle 2,3
- Xiōngbù Jiǎo: Level 1,2,3/ Angle 2,3,4
- Gēn Jiǎo: Level 1,2,3/ Angle 2,3,4
- Zhou: Level 1,2/ Angle 2,3
- Xīgài: Level 1,2,3/ Angle 3,4

- Tóu: Level 1,2/ Angle 1

Defenses (Fángyù): Defenses can be applied in 3 levels and within 3 angles.

- Wài Shǒu: Level 1,2/ Angle 1,2,3,4,5

- Zhang Shǒu: Level 1,2/ Angle 2,3

- Wài Jiǎo Fángyù: Level 2,3/ Angle 2, 3

- Nei Jiǎo Fángyù: Level 2,3/ Angle 2, 3

- Zhou Fángyù: Level 1,2 / Angle 2

- Xīgài Fángyù: Level 3 / Angle 3

Movements: Here we include all the movements to be applied with or without the application of the previous techniques, depending on the level of the student.

- Duo Bi: Level: 1,2/ Movement: Standing

- Tuī: Level: 2/ Movement: Standing

- Hou Tui: Level: any/ Movement: backwards

- Bō: Level: 1/ Movement: Standing

- BaoZhou DuoBi: Level: 1,2/ Movement: 1,2

Training Codes

In order to interpret and decode techniques or movements, we can merely follow the next resume, created to facilitate the conception, sharing and practice of forms among practitioners of DK, therefore transforming it into an interactive and fun martial art that anyone can practice and help transform, because DK is unlimited in the amount of ways that can be applied.

Action

A - Attack

D - Defense

E - Evasive

G - Grappling

Level

1. Head

2. Torso

3. egs

Side

1. Right

2. Left

3. Both

Body

P - Hand

F - Foot

E - Elbow

K - Knee

H - Head

W - Weapon

Angle

1. Upward-vertical

2. Upward-crossed

3. Horizontal

4. Downward-crossed

5. Downward-vertical

Movement

1. Right

2. Left

3. Center

Training Chart

This chart simplifies the previous chapter.

Action	A, D, E, G
Level	1, 2, 3
Side	1, 2
Body	P, F, E, K, H
Angle	1, 2, 3, 4, 5
Movement	1, 2, 3

Here are some examples of how it applies:

D12 P32

D12 - Defense with the left hand to the head level.

P32 – Horizontal hand movement from the left-side

D11 P31

D11- Defense with the right hand to the head level

P31 - Horizontal hand movement from the right side

A12 P32

A12 – Attack with the left fist to the head

P32 – Horizontal hand movement from the left-side

A11 P31

A11 – Attack with the right fist to the head

P31 - Horizontal hand movement from the righ side

D12 P32

D12 - Defense with the left hand to the head level

P32 - Horizontal hand movement from the left-side

A12 P53

A12 - Attack with the left fist to the head level

P53 – Down Vertical movement from front-side

D11 P31

D11 – Defense with right hand to the face

P31 - Horizontal hand movement from righ-side

A11 P53

A11 – Attack with right fist to the head

P53 – Down Vertical movement from front-side

A12 P53

A12 - Attack with left fist to the head

P53 – Down Vertical movement from front-side

A11 P53

A11 – Attack with right fist to the head

P53 – Downward movement from the front side

D12 P31

D12 - Defense with the left hand to the head

P31 - Horizontal hand movement from the right side

D11 P32

D11 – Defense with the right hand to the head

P32 - Horizontal hand movement from the left-side

Visual Etiquette

The etiquette for uniforms in DK has the following rules:

- Everyone must wear the same clothing, including the same colors;

- Practitioners mustn't wear shorts, but only trousers and a t-shirt;

- If choosing a t-shirt, all t-shirts must be in the same color and with the name of this martial art;

- The chosen colors for this martial art should be predominantly black and yellow;

- All practitioners must wear a belt with a color corresponding with their rank;

- Practitioners must have two bandages, being one used for technical training and the other to ensure that the wrist maintain a correct position.

The bandage for the wrist must be put as demonstrated with these pictures.

Start by the thumb, as shown in the picture.

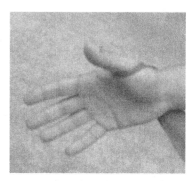

Then continue to the wrist and the pinky finger.

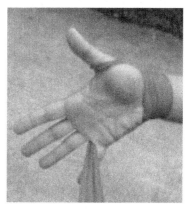

Make sure the bandage is wrapped around your wrist after passing through each finger.

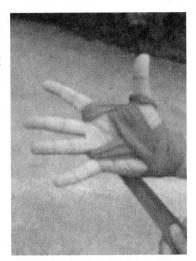

After moving near the index finger and the wrist, move it to the center of the hand to cover palm.

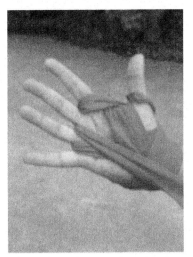

83

Finish by moving the bandage around the knuckles and wrist.

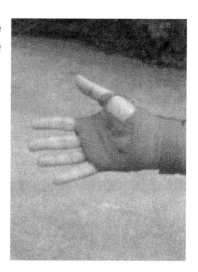

Make sure that the entire hand is well covered by the bandage and that the wrist doesn't bend. The hand and the wrist should be well aligned, which will hep you apply the techniques more effective-ly.

Rotation of   the neck and waist: Start by rotating your neck to both sides. Then do the same with the waist, first from a normal position and then lower.

Rotation of   the shoulders, elbows and wrists: Rotate your shoulders, elbows and wrists as shown in the picture.

Have particular attention when rotating the wrists, as you should force them as much as possible during the warm-up in order to avoid injuries while practicing the techniques.

Rotation of the knees: The rotation of the knees is another special part of the training and should be done as shown in the pictures, first towards the inside and then the outside.

Rotation of the feet: First, rotate your feet on the floor.

Then hold one in your hands and create pressure inward and outward, as shown in the pictures.

92

Stretching of the legs on the floor: The stretching of the legs must be applied as shown in the pictures and without insistences. It must be applied in a passive manner to avoid injuries. In each stretching, breathe in while lifting your arms up, and then out while moving your back forward and hold the position for at least 10 seconds.

Repeat the same routine two times for each position, first with both legs joined in the front, then with one leg bended and thirdly with one leg on top of another.

The fourth routine is made keeping an angle of 90° between your back knee and front leg. Finish this exercise with both legs in the front and at the same distance as your shoulders.

Stretching of the legs from a standing position: This exercise has the same purpose as the previous, with the exception that now the leg should in the same level as your waist. A table in the house should allow the same training presented in the picture. Do this exercise first as if performing a front kick, then side kick and finally back kick.

Squats: Do this exercise first with both legs joined together and the heels lifted. Then point the feet outwards and open the legs for the next round of squats as shown in the picture. Do 20 squats for each position.

Push-ups: Start with 10 push-ups putting your hands aligned with the shoulders.

Do 10 more forming a triangle with your hands.

Have a break and then repeat the triangular push-ups. Without changing the position, join your hands and do 10 more push-ups. Finish the routine by doing 10 push-ups using only the fingers.

Abdominals: Applying the position shown in the picture, stretch your legs together in the air and move them up and down 10 times.

From the previous position, do scissors, by crossing the stretching legs in an alternate way (first putting the right up and then the left) 10 times. Then, move the legs up and down while stretched, like in the first exercise, but in an alternate way 10 times. Finish with bicycle movements in the air 20 times.

As shown in the picture, push your legs together backward and forward 10 times. Finish with more bicycle movements (20 times).

Endurance: Do first 20 abdominals with your legs resting in a chair and touch the opposite knee with your shoulder every time you go up. Then do 20 push-ups backwards with the help of the same chair.

Stretching the muscles: Lay down on the floor and stretch first forward and then backward according to the exercise shown in the pictures.

Do each position 2 times.

Flexibility – Part 1: Start the exercise as shown in the first picture, with the back foot in an angle of 90º with your front foot. Insist with your weight by moving forward 5 times towards your front leg. Then do the same with the other.

Now, place your foot chest on the floor as shown in the second picture and insist in the muscle of the back-leg 5 times with the knee pointing forward, and do the same with the other leg.

In this exercise, put the top of your back foot on the ground and lift the back leg up, in order to stretch other muscles.

Bend your body outside and put your hand on the floor for balance, forcing the inside muscle of the front leg.

In the end, put both hands on the floor while keeping your legs stretched and supported on the heels, as shown in the picture, and slowly bend your body forward and backward.

Flexibility – Part 2: Using a wall as support for balance, or a tree, do the following exercises, as shown in the pictures above. Move your leg upwards and downwards in front of the torso 10 times. Then, do the same type of movement but sideways.

Repeat the previous exercise with the leg moving backwards.

Then, move the leg in a 90° angle with the rest of your body, as described in the picture.

Stretching the waist: Grab a tree or pole and bend your waist to the right and to the left, sideways and backward.

116

Jumping: Start this exercise by jumping 20 times with both legs parallel to each other and keeping your shoulders flexible.

Then jump with one leg in the front and the other in the back. Finish by jumping with your knees pointing up and alternating between them.

Biomechanical Training: The purpose of this exercise is to train the movement of the arms in the same way as it is applied for the techniques in DK. You can use a broomstick for this exercise. Start by rotating the stick in a descending form while keeping your arms next to your chin. Make sure you rotate well all of your body during the movement and not just the arms. And repeat the same movement by moving your legs forward and backward while doing it.

121

Do now ascending rotations. And finish this routine with descending and ascending rotations in x.

Shadow Boxing: Finish your warm-up practicing all the techniques, one by one, first with a rope, and then shadow boxing, without any rope, as shown in these images.

End the exercise practicing the techniques in a door entrance, a tree, a wall or a pole. Do it was well while blindfolded.

Training Levels

The levels for both solo training and class training follow the principles mentioned here. In each level a new concept is introduced into the practice, so that the student can adjust more easily.

Levels for Movement:

Level 1: Practice the techniques without moving the legs;

Level 2: Practice the techniques while doing triangular movements;

Level 3: Practice sequences of techniques in every angle, including your back;

Level 4: Blindfolded Training.

Levels for Sequences:

Level 1: Train each technique individually;

Level 2: Apply sequences with 3 techniques;

Level 3: Apply sequences with 6 techniques;

Level 4: Apply sequences of 12 techniques.

Levels for Techniques:

Level 1: Practice with legs on level 1 and 2, as well as hands, feet and elbows from a stable stance;

Level 2: Practice with legs on level 3, as well as grapples and knees, using triangular movements;

Level 3: Apply the known head attacks;

Level 4: Practice for all angles and sides.

Levels for Group Classes:

Level 1: Use of sticks to train defenses and evasives, as well as pads to practice counterattacks;

Level 2: Coordinated exercises with gloves;

Level 3: Sparring limited to 3 attacks;

Level 4: Free sparring with protective gear..

Rank Examination

The student is evaluated according to the following items:

1. Showing each attack, defense, grapple and evasive in an individual manner, as shown in the pictures of this book;

2. Showing fight sequences alone, in which first he demonstrates the attacks and then the defenses, or both at the same time when being examined for black belt;

3. In each rank, the student must do the sequences corresponding to his level and also the ones of the previous levels;

4. Showing fight sequences with a partner that applies both the defenses and attacks;

5. Free fighting with protective gear;

The following fight sequences present the complete program from beginner to Instructor level. There are four levels presented, not including the black-belt, which must be acquired and certified with the founder. The sequences are presented with the codes mentioned in this book.

Each column refers to the role of one of the two students in the fight.

WHITE BELT	
A12P-KH13*	E-Avoiding
A22F13	D21E31
A11E21	D12E53
A31F21	D31F21

*KH=knife hand

GREEN BELT	
Defend	Grab the right arm
A12P32	D12E52
A11P21	D12E51
A12P12	D12P22
Defense for grappling	Grab the left hand wrist with the right hand

A21F23	D21P32
A12F21	D12E51
A32F23	D12F23
Defense for grappling	Grab the shirt with the left hand
A22K32	D21E22
A31K31	D32K32
A22K32	D21K32
Defense for grappling	Grab the shirt on the left-shoulder-with the right-hand
A11E21	D12E51
A12E32	D11E52
A11E21: attack with another arm simultaneously protecting the counter attack.	D11E21: defend and use elbow for the counter attack.

BLUE BELT

Defense for grappling	Grab the neck with the left hand
A11P31	Wave to the left side
A32P53	D31P22
Backwards-A11P32	Wave to the right side
	Grab the shirt with both hands and project the opponent using the body as leverage
Defend in the same way, with arms crossed.	Grab the front of the shirt with both hands again, but this time allow the defense to occur.

Use a backward rotation with the right foot heel in level 2	D21P32
A21F13	D22P31
A22F11	Avoiding

BROWN BELT

A10H13	Avoiding to the right side
D12E51	
A11P23	A10H32
D22E21	D12E51
A11E23	A21K33
D32K32	D12E51
	A31K53

A12P23	D11E52
D11E52	A12E23

Grab the neck with both hands for A10H13	Stop the movements with both arms in the face and back-kick to the groin.
Twist your body to avoid being hit by the kick and apply one grappling-defense, finishing it by pushing the opponent way.	
End with a double spin-kick at Level 1 from the right to the left.	The opponent does the same movement at the same time and in the same direction (from left to right).

Training Program

- Follow the warm-up program mentioned in this book;
- Start the technical training with a rope;
- Practice shadow boxing for all techniques, including attacks, defenses, grapples and evasives;
- From a stable stance, use the rope to practice one defense followed by one attack;
- Then with triangular movements, use the rope to practice one defense followed by one attack;
- Practice all the techniques while moving forward and backwards;
- Practice the fight sequences according to your rank, which should match your experience.

Increasing Your Chi

The following sequence is part of the training in DK and helps you relax the body and muscles after the workout, while unblocking the chi in your body by using acupuncture principles. Use your fingers to massage the neck, head and arms in clockwise movements, as described in the images.

Use the thumbs to massage the intersection between the neck and back of the head. Then change the position of the hand to create pressure in the opposite direction. And finish by doing the same routine in the region below your hears.

134

Use one hand to grab the trapezius and massage it using the hand in the form of a shell. Then do the same on the other side.

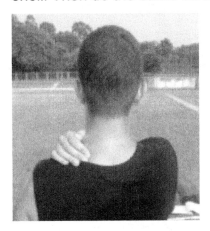

Massage the upper part of your throat.

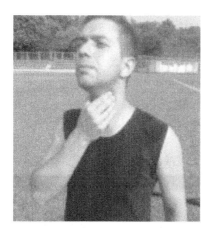

Apply clockwise movements with pressure in your front lobes;

Massage the muscles on your arm with clockwise movements. Continue doing the same until you reach your wrist and hand.

Using the knuckles to massage the back

Twist your wrists next to your spine and in its direction. Then do the same next to your waist.

Apply clockwise movements in the direction of your spine from outside to inside. Then, apply movements as if you were digging inside the spine. Repeat the same exercise in the opposite direction.

Go up and down, circling your wrists next to your spine and following in the same direction.

Simulating the Blood Circulation

With your hand open to slap your leg and arms from the upper muscles down and then up. Do the same in your chest with your hand closed.

Instructors of DK

In order to practice this martial art, you should receive a recommendation from a specialized doctor about your health. It's not a martial art for anyone but for healthy people. Therefore, be sure as well to be careful during the application of the exercises mentioned here, as they should be performed as shown, and if possible under the surveillance of a certified instructor.

The author of this book cannot be responsible for any misuse and bad application of the information provided, as they merely follow common exercises also applied by himself for years in his own personal workout.

Above all, it's important to mention that this book intends to be a self-defense manual allowing the opportunity to practice alone and at home.

Regarding the possibility of teaching Danmar Kung Fu, anyone with this book is allowed to have a training group as an independent and uncertified Instructor, if this manual is literally followed in every detail mentioned regarding the practice and the levels.

The title of certified instructor is reserved to those that receive the diploma directly from the founder.

If you hold an Instructor certification from any other martial art, you can apply to be a Danmar Kung Fu Instructor simply by sending videos of your performance to the founder for evaluation.

The knowledge exposed in this book and this martial art should always be respected. If you intend to show the techniques and training procedures here mentioned you must name the source of it or its founder, because the concept of training and fighting demonstrated in this book is unique and copyrighted.